ZEPHYR'S WHISPER

Poems and Parables of a Seasonal Pretense

Poetry by

Ken Allan Dronsfield

Scarlet Leaf

2018

©Copyright, All Rights Reserved

Cover Photo from Pixabay.com formatting by the author.

SCARLET LEAF PUBLISHING HOUSE

TORONTO ONTARIO CANADA

COPYRIGHT BY KEN ALLAN DRONSFIELD

ISBN: 978-1-988827-69-8

No part of this book can be used or reproduced in any manner whatsoever without written permission, except in the case of brief quotations embodied in critical articles and reviews.

For information address:

Scarlet Leaf Press

  scarletleafpublishinghouse@gmail.com

Table of Contents

Author's Commentary 9
Whispers from the Zephyr 12
A Morning's Calling 13
Sonnet #2, Adieu, Sonnet to the Rain 15
A Melting 16
A Fehér Hattyú (The White Swan) 17
A Turning of the Swale 19
A Timeless Splendor 21
Where Tall Trees Dance 23
White Silk and Whispers 24
With Charcoal Black 25
Briers and Brambles 26
Dérive (Drift) 27
Footprints 29
Into the Rye 30
Resonance 32
Rêves de soie (Silk Dreams) 33
Rusty Wet Leaves 34
Solstice at Christmas 35
Spanish Moss Sways 37
Sunday Smile 39
Sonnet #10, The Deer Crossing 40
Torn Sails 41
Turquoise Heart 42
The Leaves Wink 43

While the Wind Howls	44
Sail into Eternity	46
Shimmers	47
Tranquility Point	48
Sonnet #23, Tear in the Autumn Moon	49
The Ebb and Flow	50
The Old Hound at Christmas	51
Whisper of the Raven	53
Winter's Wake	54
A Velvet Rhapsody	56
A Reddish Haze	57
Bestowed Blessings in a Harvest Sonnet	58
Corn Stalk Scarecrow	59
Desert Spirit	61
Firefly	63
Golden Locks	64
Just a Dream	65
Of Mountains and Meadows	66
Pacific Daydream	67
Sighs of Serenity	69
Song of the Garden Chimes	70
Spring Will Soon Spring	71
Strawberry Daiquiri & Silk Roses	73
Au Revoir to Summer	74
A Warmer Veil	75
Sonnet #3, Earth Cries; Heaven Smiles	76
A Violet Sheen	77

Crispy Stars & Smoky Clouds	79
Bug Opus	80
Final Gasp	82
Kiss of the Hummingbird	83
Raven's Flavor	84
Spring Solstice	85
Sunrise Whispers	86
A Stellar Ballet - (Villanelle Poetry Form)	88
The Lyrical Swells	90
With Honesty Comes the Rain	91
Brooding of Night	93
Sonnet 103, Rose and Thistle	94
DEDICATION	96
AUTHOR'S BIOGRAPHY	98

Author's Commentary

I want to take a moment to thank the many wonderful people I've met since beginning my poetry career. Thank you to Roxana Nastase, Editor in Chief of the Scarlet Leaf Review and Scarlet Leaf Publishing for supporting my poetry and the work of other poets throughout the world. It is with the support of people like Roxana, Raja Williams, CEO of Creative Talents Unleashed and so many others that keep me writing and evolving into a contemporary poet. My first published poetry collection is "The Cellaring" a book containing 80 works of a light horror, paranormal, haunted, weird and wonderful poems. My second collection, "A Taint of Pity", contains life poems of a cracked inflection. A little eccentric and eclectic poetry all with a message contained within each piece. They can be purchased through Amazon.com.

I would also like to thank my dear friend Michael Lee Johnson for 'lighting the fire' which has put me on the path to publishing my work all over the globe. To date, I'm published in 24 countries and currently have 1460 published poems in the last two plus years. Michael and I have just completed our third poetry anthology,

"Warriors with Wings" which will be available through Amazon soon. The other two, "Moonlight Dreamers of Yellow Haze" and "Dandelion in a Vase of Roses" are currently available through Amazon.com. With that, I'll close with the comment, "Keep reading and writing Poetry. Keep it Alive! Enjoy My Work!

Ken Allan Dronsfield

Whispers from the Zephyr

Sugar cane flowing like ocean waves
Florida winds blow as egret's hunt lunch
tapestry woven in a wildness of saw grass
buzzards perch high on branches of oak
dragonflies rest on blades of palmetto
unscrupulous clouds build to a zephyr
horizontal rains pelt all within the glades
saunters by quickly; sun now reappears.
Spanish moss drips from Cypress trees
curtains of humidity hold a damp grip
songbirds fluttering, the gators cruising;
in the great Florida swamp; days roll by;
a muskrat swims in the calming waters
a pinkish haze envelops the twilight sky
Great Blue Herons stand at stoic repose;
Listen to the whispers from the zephyr.

A Morning's Calling

Sleep with stars orbiting your mind

bees nap while dreaming of flowers.

Old rooster sits upon the barn roof

a clear view of the fields of fantasy.

Back porch light attracts VW Bugs

moon but a sliver of icy humble pie.

Illusion of literality with fruitfulness

rise from the feather bed for coffee.

Field mouse dines on feta cheese

the alarm clock's spring has sprung

morning glows in a very special way

a burnt orange, with purple and reds.

Rooster now crows, and we're awake

the old farm whispers upon the breeze.

Stories are told of lives come and gone

sitting on the porch, breakfast is ready.

Eggs, coffee, sliced ham and potatoes

coveting an idiom of morning's calling.

Sonnet #2, Adieu, Sonnet to the Rain

The raindrops fall with enchanted magic
spattering upon that old metal roof
a melodious rhythmic sleeping tune
my tired lips welcome steeping ginseng tea
I crave soft pillows and comforter to
carry me off to my sweet restful dreams.
The hound is fed and warming by the fire
candles now smolder a wispy goodnight.
My robe and slippers rest near the bedside.
Slide deep into heaven, cat at my feet.
Sleep well sings the bashful yawning new moon,
Tap, tap, tap chant the raindrops on the roof.
This evening ends as a cherished sonnet.
Stars whisper soft to me, adieu, adieu.

A Melting

winter storm of inglorious snow
finding a home in higher lands
melting to the harmonious tune
slowly cascades in an icy rush.
granite rocks and rough water
telling tales of whetted trails
journey to the depth of oceans
from wood, swamp and glade.
pious path of fearless doubt
wildflower's hum in rhymes
seers decree honored vows
life giving legacy to all about.
reverent thoughts move along
scowls and frowns devoid here
beauty and mystique whisper
a mountain melting carries on.

A Fehér Hattyú (The White Swan)

On the small lake outside of Budapest

a sunny Sunday morning and cloudless sky

the old swan takes her final breath as

the cat nine tails bow in solemn silence.

As her life slowly slips away, a single small

white cloud appears, a vision of her mate

taken by a fox some years ago circles,

the lonely old white swan slowly dies

No one comes to pay their respects

cat nine tails bow with a feted grace

the weeping willows shed unseen tears

and the old swan takes a final breath

Mallards fly by, and the hawks stay high

painted turtles glide as grasses sway

whilst children stand on the bank and cry,

church bells sound in the distant valley,

as old white swan gently closes her eyes.

A Turning of the Swale

I turn slightly to the left to enjoy
the warm sunshine kiss my face.

I still don't know who my mother or
father were, but that doesn't matter,
I think about it from time to time.

I always find myself with thoughts
of birds, insects, fish and harsh winds.

I rejoice as the tides rise and watch
with amazement as the little crabs
scurry about like many sugar ants
who found a leftover sweet cookie.

The cat-o-nine tails are changing
color now, from bright green to a
light brown, and looking down, I see
even now, I'm slowly feeling the

effects of Autumn; soon I'll fall away
as the sea swale turns to salt hay.

As days of this lovely fall pass by;
colors turn, not only in the great wood
but here along the marsh and tidal pools.
Ducks, shore birds and minnows now
disappear and large flocks head south.

Winter's gift of frost and snow shall
finally pass and once again we'll return
next spring as sweet sea swale grass.

A Timeless Splendor

Gnarled fingers
grasping tight;
the buttered,
black raspberry
jam covered
toasted muffin.
Sun now up; cool
morning breezes;
hot coffee quietly
awaits as does my
little chihuahua.
Slippers on with
pen and pad in hand.
Blue jays jousting
over the burnt crust.
On the back porch
watching as the dog
chases the many

hoodoos or whatsits
in the fenced yard;
soon corralled but a
barista's not here;
back inside we go;
for another cup of
timeless splendor.

Where Tall Trees Dance

It's afternoon here in the valley of wood
where tall trees dance; long walks covet
an ambiance of romance and gentle calm.
It's silent and serene; the only sound being
light snow falling; like twinkling glimmers of
diamonds hitting branches and ground.
All covered in white; and my candle is alight
on the window sill near the warming fire.
The orange glow and falling snow
elicit memories of marshmallows melting
in steamy mugs of delicious hot cocoa.
Boots, hats and scarves hang by the door.
a time to remember the beloved youthful days
and simple ways here; where tall trees dance.

White Silk and Whispers

Lazy mists envelop this land;
scarlet sky with a serene azure;
working fields of cotton or yam;
adrift within a sun dog's rapture.
Awkward stare at waltzing ravens
escape aromas; decayed river silt;
prayers come and rise to Heaven
her old wheel spins white raw silk.
A cool breeze blows over the bay,
whispers of death, the devil's desire.
Life at the crossroad relives each day,
as Robert Johnson strums in the fire.
(https://en.wikipedia.org/wiki/Robert_Johnson)

With Charcoal Black

Today I'll travel to the swamp and wood
to do a little autumn sketching for the
painting projects during the cold winter.
As I pack my thermos and bag, I see
snail trails leaving the autumn garden.

Cooler breezes beget browner grasses;
lichen and moss cover the old stone wall,
I swear a little chipmunk ran by just now.
Crows are busy in their murder covens.
The songbirds leave daily for warm skies.

Smells of the forest still musty and damp
colored leaves fall, a winters quilt woven
Ice sheets now form in the ponds as geese
happily, swim throughout coolish waters.
Frogs and turtles hibernate until spring.

A puff on the pipe, and a sip from the flask,
take out my sketch pad from the canvas bag.
Deer moving through the hemlock swamp.
It's time to capture, using a charcoal black,
the precious moments on this autumn day.

Briers and Brambles

Rambling through
the brambles as
scrub and briers
grasp upon me as
honey bees buzz
all about the brush.
Blackberry wine
dreams, while an
intoxicated mind
forever schemes.
Another splash of
Jack from the flask
in a life of fails we
keep filling the pail
with those fine ripe
sweet blackberries.

Dérive (Drift)

Look there, a lone leaf drifts in the breeze

floating down through the now bare trees

finally, land upon a bleached white skull

that has laid there since last Halloween.

Coffee pot makes its melodious growl

the old cat's tail thumps keeping time

blueberry's sit in a purple stained bowl

I wonder if you've left to go get the mail.

Thoughts, like the leaf, drift in your mind

time passes quicker than it did as a child

our little dog barks chasing a what-zit

coffee in tow, another log put on the fire.

blissful blues waft from the parlor stereo

the cat looks up as the horn section plays

you return from a walk with a hurried step

the pancakes smell wonderful, you know?

Candle on the desk flickers in the fall wind

I write another verse to that autumn poem

tossing the ink, but it doesn't sound right

breakfast awaits, we dérive to the kitchen.

Footprints

Walking on pebbles in sands of white
skyward watching as stars now peek
moon glows from a blanket of clouds
lights from ships are horizon bound.
Inviting ocean of impassioned bliss
of salty smiles and springtime hugs
admission, the price of a sand dollar
seagulls following schools of baitfish.
Dogs running free and enjoying play
evening's first star, we make a wish.
Sky of twilight in red or purple hues
serenity whispers in calming breezes.
Migrating birds slowly moving north
days are longer, and nights are warmer
timeless footprints left on sandy dunes
a lovely quiescent wispy edge of night.

Into the Rye

Warm humid nights
as clouds mark time
spirits adrift in shadows
summer dreams hushed
sporadic lightning bugs
mimic the twinkling stars
deer feed at the tree line
pond frogs sing baritone
crickets echo white noise
a bottle of wine breathes
dogs bark by the old farm
faeries patiently whisper
of haunting misty dances
bats flutter in the moonlight
rye swale bows to the wind
owls chat from barn to wood
life goes on in these meadows

hand in mine, her kiss awaits
gentle hugs, perfumed essence
wafts into a wanton tranquility.
We sit upon the quilted throw
watching a great stellar show,
here in the waving rye swale.

Resonance

Patterned pain from the lost kindred
resonance of love felt by the heartless
wanton telling of tales in lost tongue
a whistling rhyme vibrates Plato's ear.
Tasting dreams of all spoiled children
orbs adrift disappearing before dawn
a pious discontent is left in the soul
liars are often cowering underground.
Alight upon the head of a icy needle
street urchins smile for a lone dollar
a red tide abates at the lowest ebb
whirling about we simply wait to die.
Vibration causation in a feted toddy
watch lava destroy a lonely memoir
pen your lines to a summer's crush
a resonance of love just drifts away.

Rêves de soie (Silk Dreams)

In the breath of a cascading waterfall...
I hear the voices of child spirits reciting sonnets,
fallen leaves that silently land upon brown grass
weaving a colorful quilt in the wood and meadow.

Trout cruise the pools along babbling brooks in
search of small meals of worms, grubs or flies.
I watch them feed, as a lone red leaf floats by
gathering speed then disappears downstream.

Chickadee's and Nuthatches flutter in the pines
as Blue Jay's squawk at me from higher branches.
Walking the path, I feel a sting below the ear,
the seasons last mosquito has found me out here.

In the breath of a falling tide... je rêve.

Snow white sails billowing in the warm trades,
rolling seas of a turquoise blue, reflect silken clouds,
terns and gulls from tropical islands hover above.
Flying fish leap and glide as dolphins follow.

In the breath of a falling tide... je me réveille.

A thermos of hot tea sits beside me in the dunes
tall marsh grasses flow with the on-shore breeze.
I slowly sip my cup as flocks of geese fly over,
I smile, close my eyes and find myself adrift.

In the breath of a Zephyr's Whisper... Je pars.

Rusty Wet Leaves

Boots of black, whetted by rain
forgotten memory left far behind
woodpecker tapping upon birch
moss covered granite whispers
deer disappear into fern & pine
partridge drum in the deep hollow
woodland faeries smiling softly
path covered in rusty wet leaves
gentle breezes calm and serene
bear moves in undulating ripples
car horns echo in a distant valley
peaceful surrender, enchantingly.

Solstice at Christmas

Fields of mottled dead grass
rotting apples lie unclaimed
deer tracks cover the hillside
orchards are graveyard silent.
Hazy winter of graying skies
winds blowing through the trees
train whistle sounds by the river
hot coffee warms cold hands.
Chickadees and jays flutter about
wood smoke wafts in the valley.
Squirrels race on the stonewall
a lone falling snowflake cheers.
The winter solstice has spoken,
whispers in an icy crispy voice
lazy strolls on the forest paths
skipping rocks on the frozen lake.

Knitted hat and mittens welcome
days of no sunshine are a plenty
while the winter solstice smiles in
December on this Christmas Day.

Spanish Moss Sways

Porch swing moves in rhythm with gentle southern breezes.

Floorboards noisily creaking

while rocking chairs dance.

The smells of honeysuckle

and Granny's fried chicken

wafting through the fields

of peanut, cotton and okra.

Fond memories return of

Sunday's after-the-service.

Friends and peach cobbler, end the day as twilight calls.

Ducks fly by heading west,

into a tangerine colored sky.

Remembering warmer days

as the Spanish Moss sways

in gentle southern breezes

cooler nights in a haunted fog

chasing frogs in the old creek

cat fishing at the old town pond.

Sweet southern times reign as do walks in old town Savannah.

haunting timeless remembrance

the memories linger in my heart.

Sunday Smile

eggs are on the boil
stove hot and ready
cat in my old chair
toaster takes awhile
sausage and taters
frying as I dodge
splatters of grease
coffee pot beeping
cat trades for food
ready my blue plate
sun peeks over trees
I smile on Sunday's.

Sonnet #10, The Deer Crossing

Sun slowly dipping in the western sky;

the winds are light and the pine boughs tossing.

From their warm, peaceful beds the meek and shy,

walk to the river; time for the crossing.

To the fields above, to graze for a meal;

prance through the meadow, always listening.

Hear the Blue Jay; alerting all with zeal.

Just twilight now, time to make the crossing.

Squirrels have disappeared, gone to their beds.

Barn Owls glide by upon whispering wings.

Night animals stir, sleepiness now shed.

Stand on the bank, hear the cicadas sing.

Enter the cool waters, off to be fed.

Browse til dawn, then return to the crossing.

Torn Sails

Wild rambling roses of ocular bloom
salted crackers served with the tequila
worms hiding from bouncing Robins
ripple chips best to have with clam dip
swirling icy vortex of inebriated candor
toast with gin and shovel down ramen
pin stripe gray suit with a flamboyant tie.
I've lost all sight of that ruthless treason
reverent hide behind a purple pious cross
Expedia searches for a ticket to nowhere
the kibitzer only charges two cents a day
eyes shining a scarlet glow during twilight
with darkness arrives the blood red moon
the raucous dogs of war howl until sunrise
reprieve I concede as I'm left on a sandbar
adrift through a dispirited life with torn sails.

Turquoise Heart

I want to travel home to my beautiful island
where turquoise waters soothe an injured soul.
Listen and you will hear the jungles singing
songs from the past as ghostly drums echo.
Whispers dancing from hills and valleys to
the giant palms and those tall rocky cliffs.
The white sand beaches wrap around the island,
birds and small animals scatter and run about.
Searching tidal pools for tidbits or small meals
those beautiful egrets lift off into the warm breeze.
I'm ready to travel home to the beauty of my island
where the turquoise waters welcome my lost soul.

The Leaves Wink

Whispered stillness at dawn
summer candle burning low
a quieted hush upon a breeze
orange koi rise in the fountain.
Leaves wink in the sun's haze
toaster pops my English muffin
coffee pot chugs along slowly
cars roll by as the day begins.
Sirens echo in the distant hills
dogs howl and children smile
faceless people rush to a bus
lazy summer awaiting autumn.
Pumpkin patch on its final days
crispy mornings and hot cocoa
Autumn's time will soon be here;
leaves wink because they know.

While the Wind Howls

Flames reflected within the cat's eye

a glass of spirits awaits a parched soul

wool socks warming my chilled feet

the dog listens while the wind howls.

Teapot whistles in a shrieking pitch

inside a little cabin on a snowy night

as loneliness wreaks of rumination

a harsh stare from the napping cat.

Ink flows smooth on a poet's night;

imagination tickles a swirling mind

image of acute emotional darkness

seeking the shadowed voice inside.

As the cat now naps with an eye open

a mouse creeps upon the window sill

the snow shovel falls with a clamor

everyone jumps while the wind howls.

Sail into Eternity

Waves crash in timely succession
pounding sand as shorebirds run.
pelicans soar on flaming wave crests
ships at sail move slowly offshore.
Seaweed dries in the scorching sun
lover's embrace upon plaid throws
fisherman cast into the calm bay
foghorns speak from the outer isle.
Seagulls gather before the twilight
standing upon the rocks and beach.
I'm sailing off into the sunset; but
my hope is to sail off into eternity.

Shimmers

Clustering wildflowers
unkempt in meadows
alder leaves shimmer
like wings of flying teal
winding along the river
dandelions dreaming
a red rose promised
rust devours a tractor
broken old tree swing
clusters of wildflowers
by an unkempt garden
tears cry the homestead
free-falling into memory.

Tranquility Point

Walk into the sand; of a dune avalanche.
Grasses swaying to hot steamy winds;
sounds of waves crashing to shore;
seagulls bartering for tidbits in rocks
along the stagnant shallow festering,
marshy salt pools near the open sea.
Hot feet begging for the touch and
soothing sensation of chilled waters
racing from depths to chase the shore
birds and children all along the beach.
Egrets hunt minnows as twilight greets the
coolish sea breeze. Another day gone;
Tranquility Point is once again, at ease.
(Pushcart Prize Nominee, 2016 Poetry Pacific)

Sonnet #23, Tear in the Autumn Moon

Keeper of trees, au pair of great forests
please tell me why you leave bare stark branches
cold and leafless until the spring arrives?
Where are the beautiful majestic leaves
that always shade me from the harsh hot sun?
I pray the Maples are well and still sweet.
I love the beauty of dancing Alders,
their yellow leaves shimmer in the breeze of
a cool late summer's day full of sunshine.
Each day snowflakes drift down, like leaves during
autumn's call we remember the beauty
of green forests and wait for warmer days.
I'm left after winter, but on moon beams,
a willow's tear left to fade, fade away.

The Ebb and Flow

From atop the great redwood trees
dragonflies fantasize of summertime;
of warmer mornings, balmy winds
dodging flycatchers and bullfrogs.
The grass is green beside the pond
wolves howl and worship the full moon
barn owls love a midnight stellar show
baby goslings enjoy the fresh sunrise.
Beating hearts strong by marshy creeks
deep rivers and great bays ebb and flow
large animals enjoy the salty-sweet grass
wildflowers sprinkled upon rolling hills.
As the sun now rises in the eastern skies,
from within that great awakening forest
a lone cicada sings his mating sonnet
within the ebb and flow of life's circle.

The Old Hound at Christmas

Like unblown dust on the floor of seasoned oak,
he sleeps all curled up next to the old wood stove,
laying there he dreams of Christmas days gone by;
times spent chasing squirrels, hunting hoodoos and
hours of walks through the great spruce, oak and snow
looking for that perfect Christmas tree to be shown.
A bit of gray now apparent on his angelic resting face.
He walks a little slower on those colder winter days,
and always gravitates towards the warmth of the fire.
He's my faithful friend through good times or bad.
Listening to my rants at losing ball games, and all
the laughter during some great old comedy shows.
Always there watching the parades, he loves snoopy.
A protector on those dark stormy nights, a staunch

supporter when others have fallen away by and by.

And as this Christmas eve comes to an end, I am much

more nostalgic, spending these quiet moments with him.

My friend, my soul, my shadow, my old Hound.

Whisper of the Raven

Tension breaks as the last snowflake melts

we welcome those warmer days and nights

cows calmly graze in sweet green pastures

flocks of birds return to forests and waters.

Robins bounce across the fresh front lawns

lovely dandelions sprout freely giving wishes

bicycle chains are oiled and readied for rides

and we walk the shores searching for treasure.

Windows opened to freshen rooms of winter

spring rains bring cascades of wild flowers

great eagles soar above surveying the lands

Ravens whisper greetings to blooming lilacs.

Winter's Wake

Whilst I sat upon a snowflake and pondered
life that came that November, never forgotten.
The summer's wears were all safely stored in
a small barn and log cabin by the big misty lake.
My arms and hands are so worn and beaten,
filling and moving those barrels of apple cider
as blustery cold winds made my eyes teary and
the old horse slowed only to cross the icy river.
An oak walking stick plunges deep in fresh snows
my fireplace feels nice, helping flakes melt away
the feeling finally returning to fingers and toes as
an early winter shook us all upon that autumn day.
Those democrats fought during the winter's blast,
while republican's schemed in ever coolish dreams
slight of shadowed hands quickly stuffed the ballots

an evil liar did show her heart as the cold winds blew.
Whilst I whispered upon a snowflake and pondered
this January's frosty cold and our uncertain tomorrow
we're feeling a strangeness within an evening's twilight
during the colder days of a Winter's crude wake.

A Velvet Rhapsody

In the amber mists and wispy bonds;
a chilly stillness weeps in despair;
clouds fade with a morning flair and
dissolve above bare trees and pond.
The Sun fights with a pious tenacity;
burning through the coolish caress;
warming the soul without remiss,
and return the land to a passivity.
O' warming orb of stellar radiance;
watcher of time, forever descendant;
sultry trance, of a chimerical beauty;
heated passions of wanton evanescence.
Autumn's heart; reluctantly withdrawn;
the gaze upon an amber velvety haze;
Bow down and pray; a rhapsody ablaze;
to a winter solstice in the spirited dawn.

A Reddish Haze

Nocturne of shadow
rise with a Flamingo
charmed by a sunrise
a reddish haze smiles
prone upon the pillow
cherished teacup pouts
hushed morning sonnet
whispers at my window.
Dreams left to wander
my fan begins the day
humidity now departing
the sea birds serenade.
sand dunes sparkling
as diamond glints glow
grasses flow serenely
terns hover surfside
in mild on shore wind
hot water is now ready
a royal blend steeping
cherished teacup grins
my Siamese cat yawns
awaken a reddish haze.

Bestowed Blessings in a Harvest Sonnet

Pussy Willows grow at the edge of the field
cows grazing amongst brambles and berries.
Cat birds cry from a stand of shimmering Alders
breeze sways grasses like gentle ocean waves.
The Pheasant race to thickets for a safer cover
alone in the fields, I lay down and watch the sky.
The grass is warm after a day spent in the sun,
clouds racing eastward towards the Atlantic like,
huge ruffled pillows of fluffy feted marshmallows.
No butterflies dancing or dragonflies romancing,
pumpkins now orange and acorn squash ready,
corn is now cut, stalks are placed on lamp posts.
Leaves will soon be changing, bursting with color,
crowds abandon the beaches, geese move south.
Apples waiting patiently, plump and so awesome,
moon rises slowly, humming her Harvest sonnet.
Blessed be this Earth in all her glorious splendor,
whether in the midst of day or into the dark night.
Your true peace may be found watching a sunset,
but your deep wisdom is knowing whom to thank.

(2016 Pushcart Prize Award Nominee, Spirit Fire Review)

Corn Stalk Scarecrow

In a nightly show,
branches stand bare
upon a moon's glow
corn stalks bow.
A red fox sings loud
during a coolish night
within a foggy shroud
of an early October.
Frost patiently awaits,
to kiss the green grasses
and leave a wisp of white
upon amber pumpkins.
Cute chipmunks play
and store winter food
blue jays forage and stay
along walls of granite.

Corn stalks left behind
staring at the scarecrow
during the harvest time
Jack O'Lantern's smile.

Desert Spirit

With the moon rise

on a spring night,

a chilled wind flows

through my hair.

In the desert cold,

near the Joshua Tree,

the sands still warm,

from the sunny rays,

as scorpions danced

during a hot hazy day.

As our dreams recall

the age of the Phoenix

reflecting mirrors glare,

of a pious deity shared

near the Joshua Tree,

where sands are warm,

from the sunny rays,

in that desert of old,

haunted fables are told

by desert spirits today.

Firefly

You can steal away with my sun;
but never take the night sky from me.
Green the grass with gentle rains
and inspire adventures in soft breezes
keep me warm as autumn arrives
humming, "Fly Me to the Moon" while
kissing stars in a twinkling flourish.
My light will touch a child's memory
allow me life for a moment in time
cherish us as we'll be gone very soon
touching your heart again next July
that lovely luminescent waltz of a firefly.

Golden Locks

Incessant jovial mumbling aghast
golden locks upon a morning breeze
convertible top down in harsh sunlight
Siamese cat rides proud upon the dash
casting hazy shadows from stem to stern
quieted ride upon the marshmallow tires
pizza bites sizzle on the red-hot headers
as my brain awakens in a drunken stupor
crossing the plains, without fear or disdain
seeking or freaking like a two-headed clam
memories absolved of all pleasure or piety
golden locks flow upon a morning breeze.

Just a Dream

A winter night's dream
warm sun and flowers
snows melt screaming
begging for one last day.
bikes are slowly riding
beside windblown sands
boards ride upon the surf
tan bodies lay on towels.
Red convertibles cruise by
parking on the boardwalk
in a crazy, lazy warmth
of a cold night's dream.

Of Mountains and Meadows

A solitary voice whispers
in the dark of a meadow.
Small swift orbs of light
appear to float everywhere.
The moon begins to crest
atop mountains in the east
wildflowers stand proud as
bright fireflies dart all about.
Snapdragons or buttercups
brush my hollow cheeks.
swallow your feted elation,
as meadows bathe in light
behold a rising evening fairy
sitting upon pinkish clouds
awash in dancing shadows
through, aspen, pine, and oak.
Reflecting life in the Rockies,
of her mountains and meadows.

Pacific Daydream

Lofty Willows growing
    at the edge of the pond
        water buffalo graze
            among the fields of rice.
Cat birds cry in a breeze
    by grand banyan trees
        winds sway the grasses
            like long ocean waves.
Pheasant quickly dash
    to thickets for safer cover
        alone in the fields,
            I sit and watch the sky.
Grasses are now warm
    after a day spent in sunshine
        puffy clouds racing by
            heading off towards the sea.

Colorful butterflies dancing
    and dragonflies romancing
        banana now ready
            pineapple is looking fine.
Mango and papaya,
    my favorite tropical treat
        Full moon rises slowly,
            humming a twilight sonnet.

Sighs of Serenity

As a brook winds its way
from the high mountains
through a dark forest like
a long-coiled serpent.
Little falls and rapids
sing sonnets of water's
love of raucous festive
rides enroute to the sea.
From the little bridges or
logs across the creeks,
we watch with delight
as the dew Faeries skim
along the calm ponds or
gentle eddies at sunset.
Sprinkling droplets with
magic dust covering all
the flowers, grass and
leaves in trees with a
welcome drink at night.
My heart is always there;
wrapped in an icy breath
exhaled into twilight's air
Walking the pathway home
we sigh, as serenity is here.

Song of the Garden Chimes

Steal away at moon rise,
star light kisses weary eyes,
you will find your spirit drifts
upon warm spring breezes.
Songs from garden chimes
play sonnets on a Sprites harp
whispering in shaded scarlet
directly into my wanton heart.
Oceans of grass gently sway
Robin's dance by granite walls
enchanted orbs rise from trees
as squirrels give hearty chase
the Raven sits and just watches
a twilight sky envelops the soul.
Your love keeps my heart smiling,
stars flirt above the garden chimes.

Spring Will Soon Spring

Walking through corn fields of frozen dead stalks
up to the hills, the rotting apples lying unclaimed
many deer tracks cover these meadows, the old
orchards are graveyard silent as a lone crow calls.

Another cold and hazy winter of dark graying skies
winds blowing snow through the bare oak trees
off to the east a train whistle is heard by the river
my thermos of hot coffee warming cold hands.

Truly blessed, as we have so much to be thankful,
watch the chickadees and jays flutter in pine boughs.
Two squirrels are racing down the old wall of stone
as a lone falling snowflake lands soft on my cheek.

Days of Thanksgiving and Christmas are gone now,
the winter solstice whispers in a soft quivering voice.

loving a lazy long hike along the worn forest paths as
I take a little time skipping rocks on the frozen pond.

The knitted hat and scarf, so very welcome,
Grandmother made them so very many years ago.
The winter smiling it's last, as spring will soon arrive.
A blessed day in late winter, spent here on the plains

Strawberry Daiquiri & Silk Roses

Motionlessly awake, helpless and heated
desperate for breezes of a coolish content.
Fans moving air, like that of a hot hair dryer
lazily sit by the pool, watch silk roses frown.
Ice in the freezer, fruit juice from the frig
rum in the cupboard, blender waits nearby.
Fresh sliced strawberries in a bowl now rest
sweat on the brow, the mixing time is now.
Tall glass from the hutch, granny's best crystal
the noisy whirring is done, a stroke of mastery.
Walking back to the pool with a sheepish smile
drink my strawberry daiquiri, as silk roses grin.

Au Revoir to Summer

Last night's dishes wait in the sink
hot water and soap to arrive soon
cat sits nervously pondering when
his dinner will finally fill the bowl.
Summer's sun has left for Florida
chain saws echo across the valley
pumpkin looks pitiful on the porch
wish I was more skilled at carving.
Standing in the back yard alone
watching the leaves gliding down
like paper airplanes here and there
some helicopter spin to the ground.
A sense of sadness is now borne,
colder days are well on the way.
Au revoir to Summer, Bonjour Fall.
whilst I've only written a bit all day.

A Warmer Veil

The Crocus' bloom
and sing their song.
Fighting through frost
and snowy gales.
Each year they rise,
and calmly multiply.
From the cold of Winter
to Spring's warmer veil.

Sonnet #3, Earth Cries; Heaven Smiles

The white rose petals are gently falling
floating slowly down to the bare cold ground
purple lilac's open; inhale the sun
lovely essence of both waft all about.
Red ladybugs are dancing leaf to leaf
the dragonflies sit alert on a post
red robins dodging colored leaves on lawns
my old cat naps in warm sunlit windows.
Grandfathers snooze; reflect life in old chairs
our Savior kisses a cool wrinkled cheek
the children run while playing in the yard
welcome back home to the autumn solstice
whereas the earth now cries; the heaven smiles
our summer now ends, but our fall begins.

A Violet Sheen

A thrill for sure, to dance upon the Moors;
during the Spring moon on a May twilight.
Smells found there waft about the breeze;
pine needles and shimmering of leaves.

The gentle brook serenades a sweet view;
winding through grasses as trout dine upon
the masses of golden mayflies, as if on cue.
A peaceful radiance through a violet sheen.

A shy deer sneaks a peek from the forest,
within the marsh, rabbits spar with the fox.
Winner shall reap life's illustrious conquest,
another day gone upon this new equinox.

Of a mountain high; brilliant changing sky,
listening to the geese upon a final glide.

a kingfisher hovers in air; diving to a dare,
into the pond a striped minnow he's eyed.

Time spent here in this wondrous dream,
Of where we've been and what we've seen
A simple piece of earth, within the expanse
Under the joyous dance of a Violet Sheen.

Crispy Stars & Smoky Clouds

Golden stars shimmer
as lightning bugs flash,
the sun bequeaths her last,
red sky and clouds ablaze.
Timeless splendor begets
serenity with true ardor as
twilight bells chime loudly
ending a peaceful day in time.
Egret's fly to their nesting tree
beyond the beach and sands;
moon rises fulfilling a destiny
of shadows twixt sea and land.
Gull's dance on a wave's crest
as the tide rises so very proud;
sand castles gently wash away
under crispy stars & smoky clouds.

Bug Opus

Late afternoon
setting sun relents
end of day arrives
gone much too soon
the heart beats on
as wings of a Swan
the moon rising high
light shimmers dancing
night troubadours sing
dew faeries waltzing
my cat prowls a field
cold can of lager beer
munch a hot pretzel
walk along the shore
owl hoots from pines
bug opus in white noise
distant howling calls

haunting I walk faster
homeward bound, soon
spooked cat follows close.

Final Gasp

impatiently waiting for twilight's final gasp
late summer heated night slowly emerges
breezes of lightness bend grasses so soft
ducks needing rest land upon the bay.
lighting a Camel and watch the smoke rise
in a star filled sky of a darkish purple haze
sit on the porch as the small waves crest
while an airliner high in the sky heads east.
citronella is lit as mosquito's now swarming
a full moon reaches towards a nervous sky
drifting in thought like a misty fog passing
in a blink of an eye, candle wicks dance.
life brings to boil memories of lost time
years spent without in a world full of with
cascades of dreams or fantasies live on
derelict of mind, hated even unto the sky.

Kiss of the Hummingbird

Desperate for warm bountiful seasons
search for harmony with gifted wings
dancing in the winds of roses in bloom
seen by some but touched by very few.
A duel carried on with the honey bees
a call for the taste of the sweet nectar
waltz in the sun during warmer days,
my lips feel a kiss of the hummingbird.
During warmer rains, wings swiftly beat
within the tiny nest near the raptor tree
the little bird smiles, protected so well
now twilight reigns, end of the long day.

Raven's Flavor

Coffee pot perks to the morning beats
trash cans set out along the lane
cars and trucks rumble down the road
children spy the fresh donuts smiling.
Blue Jays spar in the old lilac bush
leaves of color float from the heights
Raven's flock in a golden unkindness
Bluto the cat just lays there and naps
Maples adorned with old wood pails,
nectar to syrup for my lovely pancakes,
fresh apples rest in baskets on the porch
a last tomato ripens in a sunlit window.
tinkling of spoons in hot coffee mugs
kids laugh running to the school bus
pumpkin proudly sits upon my steps
a Raven's Fall is my favorite flavor.

Spring Solstice

Journey over time
end of a rainbow, end of a branch
plying of rhyme.
Clouds float by
adrift in a breeze, adrift through life
coursing onward.
Rainbow sleeps
edge of the day, edge of the night
now twilight time.
Spring has come
warm is the sun, warm is the heart
blooming smiles.

Sunrise Whispers

Soon a sunrise will ignite
a wispy, darkened corner
of planet Earth awakens,
warming blanket spreads
as the King of Light rises,
the unseen now revealed.

Soon surging water will
fill inland marshes and
salty tidal creeks as blue
crabs roam; shorebirds
scatter all about the sand
while seeking small meals.

Soon, chased from beaches
in a raucous rushing surf
by greedy pursuing waves.
Neptune's coveted trinkets

from the deep will safely be
kept from view forever.

Soon I'll awaken to songbirds
just outside my sunlit window.
The teapot sings a sonnet
announcing this new day of
'Sine qua non', my praise be
but an alluring whisper here.

~'Sine qua non', Latin meaning, "Something considered essential."

A Stellar Ballet - (Villanelle Poetry Form)

Time's not sleeping but forever creeping
Breathe to live while the blood is steeping,
in shadow dreams lies incessant weeping.

Heart beats as a clock, a tick and the talk
love burns with a flame in an all-night stalk
Time's not sleeping but forever creeping.

a moon rising high in this fleeting twilight.
in a teary haze, whilst affixing my sight
in shadow dreams lies incessant weeping.

Love kind and true, now absent and ablaze,
the full moon exhales within a lunar phase
Time's not sleeping but forever creeping.

unto a midnight waltz, as feelings decay
stars twinkle and whisper in a stellar ballet
in shadow dreams lies incessant weeping.

How starved your wicked ego has been,
to devour my heart with a treacherous grin.

Time's not sleeping but forever creeping
in shadow dreams lies incessant weeping.

The Lyrical Swells

Starlight stirs my coffee

The moon a soft croissant

the milky way wins my favor

A tidal ebb in a moon's glance.

Impassioned sea of lyrical swells

sunny haze and sands in rhyme.

biscuits aligned on a silk doily

the hot black tea steeps alone.

January's crispy cold begone

Leaf buds impatient to open

Twinkling orbs fill a night sky

the sea rolls to a lyrical swell.

With Honesty Comes the Rain

As horse hooves pound

upon hard clay and rock trail

dusty, water stained curtains

move in gentle humid breezes.

Thunder reigns o'er the lands

off in the distant mountains

here, it's quiet, tough to breathe

spiders tiptoe across the table.

Glistened tears fall in puddles

swollen red eyes pray for tissues

old friendships dissolve away

without any rhyme or reason.

In these lands, forgotten by many

remembered only of dirt and heat,

never ending dust rising skyward

a dust bowl of hell on earth.

Laughter is simply reflected with

dark thoughts or nightmares.

A casting of dull sun and shadow,

with honesty comes the rain.

Brooding of Night

Of limpet and crumpet
and other peculiar things.
Brooding in a chorus or
humming upon the verse.
At rest nea a bedside table
as wicked candles flicker
shadows found lounging in
darkness of the cold cellar.
Questioned a truth upheld
as sea eagles wings whistle
on tempests in graying skies.
While limpets and crumpets,
goblins and grand toadstools
await the damp chill of night.

Sonnet 103, Rose and Thistle

The instrument of a torture is said
to be born of a rose and thorns at dawn
evil briers or brambles grasping tightly
a deep snort of peppermint snuff to calm.
Alight on a box of reddish apples
or resting on a bed of fresh thistle
working knives always sharper with the sun
grievously pray on a boars head.
raw sand and salt of ravaged ocean rocks
the truth seamless or strewn in a tempest
albeit whispers speak shallow of plot.
cherish as the old man's limping footsteps
do quickly scuff along hither and yon
while gathering the red rose and thistle.

DEDICATION

This poetry collection is dedicated in memory of my Uncle, Neil Moore. My uncle took me on a wild ride into the woods when I was about 8 years old. Taking me hiking, fishing and hunting. He was a lobster fisherman and I went with him just about every day after he got home from work, I helped pull the traps, bait them and was just there to help. I spent many hours on that boat watching nature in all her glory. Birds, seals, fish and other wildlife was right there before me and I took it all in. We went trout fishing in old brooks and ponds all over the State of New Hampshire where I watched pine martens, foxes and deer. I then went with him deer hunting and once again, was always watching nature from the squirrels and chipmunks running along stone walls, to deer slowly walking through the swamps. I heard the early morning scream of a Bobcat and watched Fisher cats romping around a beaver dam. I heard the slap of the Beavers tail on the old pond and the honking of geese along the great marshes near our town. Neil has passed away now but the memories he provided me with still are fresh in my mind and are forever recorded in these poems.

Thank you, Uncle Neil, God Bless you and I still hear you say, "look Kenny look" as deer, hawks, geese or pheasant come into my view even today.

AUTHOR'S BIOGRAPHY

Ken Allan Dronsfield is a disabled veteran, poet and fabulist originally from New Hampshire, now residing on the plains of Oklahoma.

His work can be found in magazines, journals, reviews and anthologies. He has two poetry books, "The Cellaring" a collection of 80 poems of light horror, paranormal, weird and wonderful work.

His newest book, "A Taint of Pity: Life Poems Written with a Cracked Inflection just released on Amazon.com. He is a three time Pushcart Prize and twice Best of the Net Nominee for 2016-2017.

Ken loves writing, thunderstorms, walking in the woods at night and spending time with his cats Willa and Yumpy.

*Thank you for reading **Zephyr's Whisper**. If you enjoyed the poems, please, consider leaving a review or telling your friends. Word of the mouth is a poet's best friend.*

www.ingramcontent.com/pod-product-compliance
Lightning Source LLC
Chambersburg PA
CBHW070155080526
44586CB00015B/2003